Your name

This is your book.

Stewart, Tabori & Chang
New York

You were born on this day…

Date

Monday   Tuesday   Wednesday   Thursday   Friday   Saturday   Sunday

Circle one

at this time...

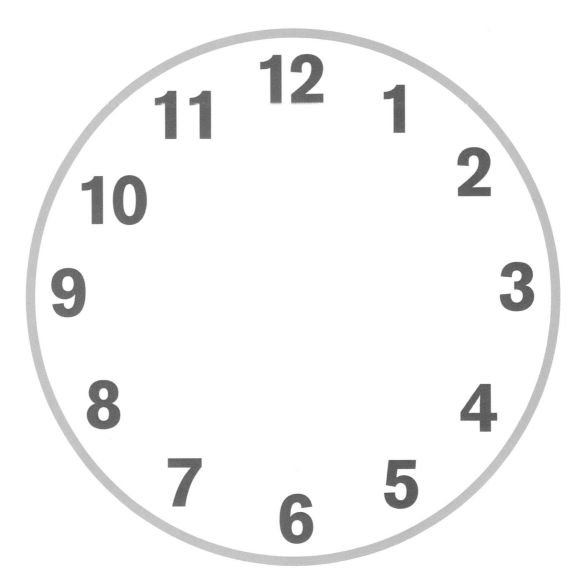

Insert hour and minute hands

A.M.　　P.M.

Circle one

You were born on this planet...

Select one

Mercury   *Venus*   *Earth*   *Mars*   *Jupiter*

Saturn   *Uranus*   *Neptune*

You were born in this country...

Select one

and in this state...

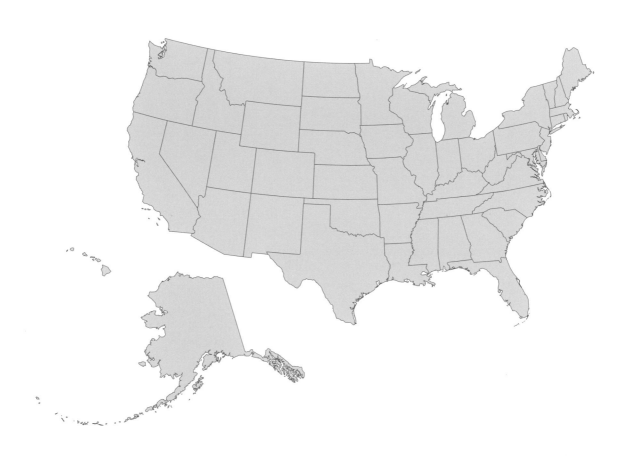

in this county...

_____

County name

in this city...

_____

City name

at this hospital...

_____

Hospital name

and this was your doctor...

_____

Doctor's signature

Here's a copy of your birth certificate…

Place copy of birth certificate here

You weighed this much…

Weight

You were this tall…

Height

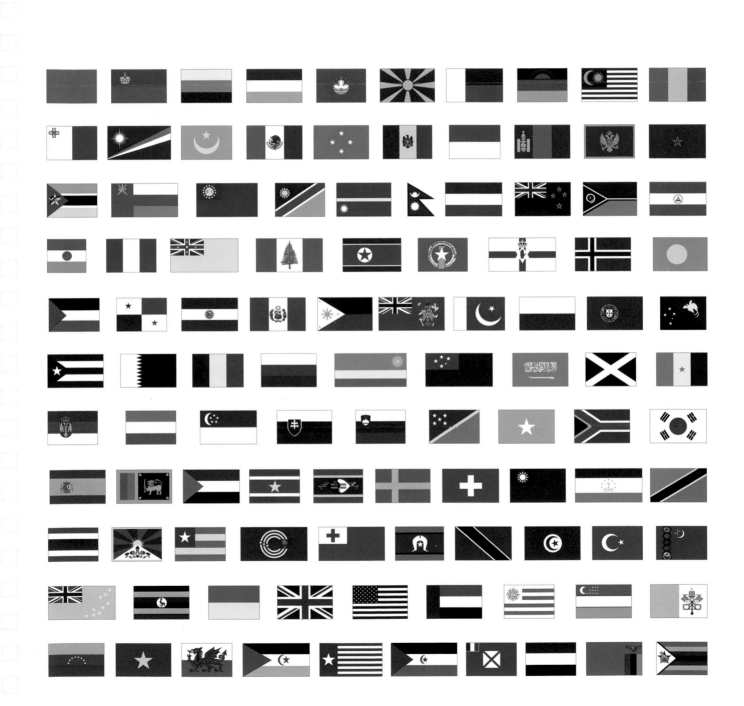

Your astrological sign is…

Circle one

ARIES　　　　**TAURUS**　　　　**GEMINI**　　　　**CANCER**

LEO　　　　**VIRGO**　　　　**LIBRA**　　　　**SCORPIO**

SAGITTARIUS　　　　**CAPRICORN**　　　　**AQUARIUS**　　　　**PISCES**

Your birth stone is...

Circle one

GARNET

AMETHYST

AQUAMARINE

DIAMOND

EMERALD

PEARL

RUBY

PERIDOT

SAPPHIRE

OPAL

TOPAZ

TURQUOISE

This is what you looked like
before you were born…

Place ultrasounds here

This is what you looked like
when you were born…

Place hospital photo here

Before you were born, there were lots of parties held in your honor…

Place baby shower invitations and photos here

We hope you like your name, because here are some of the other names that your mother considered…

_____

Name

_____

Name

_____

Name

_____

Name

_____

Name

_____

Name

and here are some names that
your father considered…

_____

Name

_____

Name

_____

Name

_____

Name

_____

Name

_____

Name

These are some thoughts
that mommy and daddy had about you
before you were born…

_____

_____

_____

_____

_____

_____

_____

_____

_____

_____

_____

_____

These are some thoughts
that mommy and daddy had about you
immediately after you were born…

_____

_____

_____

_____

_____

_____

_____

_____

_____

_____

_____

_____

This is your family tree...

These are your parents...

Place photos here

These are your grandparents…

Place photos here

These are your godparents…

Place photos here

These are your aunts and uncles…

Place photos here

These are your cousins…

Place photos here

These are the names of some
of the nice people who babysat you...

_____

Name

_____

Name

_____

Name

_____

Name

_____

Name

_____

Name

This is a picture of your first house…

Place photo here

This is a picture of you in your first Halloween costume…

Place photo here

This is a picture of you
with Santa Claus…

Place photo here

This a picture of you
in your mom's favorite outfit…

Place photo here

This a picture of you
in your dad's favorite outfit…

Place photo here

This was the big story in the news on the day you were born…

Place news clippings here

The President of the United States
the year you were born was…

_____

Washington   Adams   Jefferson   Madison   Monroe   Adams   Jackson

Van Buren   Harrison   Tyler   Polk   Taylor   Fillmore   Pierce

Buchanan   Lincoln   Johnson   Grant   Hayes   Garfield   Arthur

Cleveland   Harrison   Cleveland   McKinley   Roosevelt   Taft   Wilson   Harding

Coolidge   Hoover   Roosevelt   Truman   Eisenhower   Kennedy   Johnson   Nixon

Ford   Carter   Reagan   Bush   Clinton   Bush   Obama   other

Circle one, and ask mommy and daddy who the President was when they were born

When you were born…

the Vice President of the United States was…

_____
Name

the Speaker of the House of Representatives was…

_____
Name

the U.S. Secretary of State was…

_____
Name

the U.S. Secretary of the Treasury was…

_____
Name

the U.S. Secretary of Defense was…

_____
Name

When you were born, these were the Justices of the Supreme Court...

Chief Justice

Justice

Justice

Justice

Justice

Justice

Justice

Justice

Justice

When you were born…

the Prime Minister of England was…

_____

Name

the President of Russia was…

_____

Name

the President of China was…

_____

Name

the Prime Minister of Japan was…

_____

Name

the Governor General of Canada was…

_____
Name

the President of France was…

_____
Name

the President of Italy was…

_____
Name

the Chancellor of Germany was…

_____
Name

When you were born…

the Nobel Peace Prize Laureate was…

_____

Name

the Pope was…

_____

Name

the Dalai Lama was…

_____

Name

the Secretary General of the United Nations was…

_____

People magazine's "Sexiest Man Alive" was…

_____

the world's top female supermodel was…

_____

When you were born, there were this many people in the United States of America…

Number of people

and there were this many people in the world…

When you were born...

there were this many countries...

Number of countries

there were this many U.S. states...

Number of states

there were this many democracies in the world...

Number of democracies

there was this much
carbon dioxide in the atmosphere…

Parts per million

there were this many billionaires…

Number of people

this many people survived on less than $1 per day…

Number of people

When you were born,
these countries had nuclear weapons…

Circle those that apply

_____
Country

_____
Country

_____
Country

_____
Country

_____
Country

_____
Country

_____
Country

_____
Country

_____
Country

_____
Country

and these countries were at war…

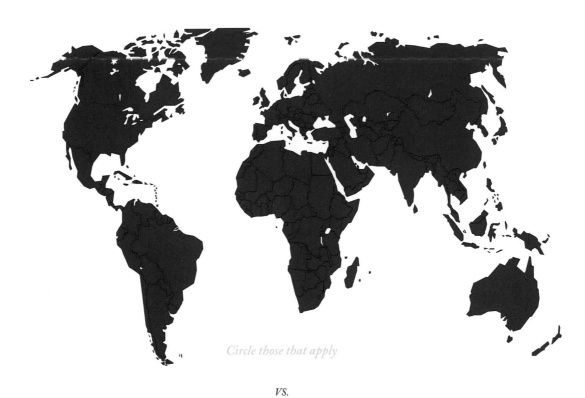

Circle those that apply

	VS.	
Country		*Country*
	VS.	
Country		*Country*
	VS.	
Country		*Country*
	VS.	
Country		*Country*
	VS.	
Country		*Country*

When you were born…

the Dow Jones Industrial Average was…

_____

Points

the NASDAQ Index was…

_____

Points

the S&P 500 Index was…

_____

Points

the Federal Funds Rate was…

_____

Percent

the U.S. Dollar to Euro exchange rate was…

Dollars/Euros

the U.S. Dollar to British Pound rate was…

Dollars/Pounds

U.S. imports were valued at…

Dollars

U.S. exports were valued at…

Dollars

When you were born…

an average computer had this much memory…

Gigabytes

the longest nonstop commercial flight was…

City to city, miles traveled, number of hours

the tallest building in the world was…

Name, country, city, height

the largest urban area in the world was…

Name, country, population

When you were born, people listened to music on one of these…

Circle one, and ask mommy and daddy what people listened to music on when they were born

When you were born, music was stored on one of these…

Circle one, and ask mommy and daddy what people stored music on when they were born

When you were born, the top five Fortune 500 companies were…

Company name

Company name

Company name

Company name

Company name

and the top five Global 500 companies were…

Company name, country

Company name, country

Company name, country

Company name, country

Company name, country

When you were born...

a bottle of water cost...

Dollars

a gallon of milk cost...

Dollars

a gallon of gas cost...

Dollars

a barrel of oil cost...

Dollars

a Starbucks coffee cost…

Dollars

a McDonald's Big Mac cost…

Dollars

a movie ticket cost…

Dollars

a baseball game bleacher ticket cost…

Dollars, stadium

When you were born...

a six-pack of beer cost...

_____

Dollars, brand

a pack of diapers cost...

_____

Dollars, brand

a thirty-second commercial during
the Super Bowl cost...

_____

Dollars

a letter stamp cost...

_____

Cents

a standard family car cost…

the median price of an American home was…

a four-year college education
at a state university cost…

a four-year college education
at a private university cost…

Here are the sports champions from the year you were born…

NFL Champions

NHL Champions

MLB Champions

NBA Champions

Master's Champion

Wimbledon Champions

European League Soccer Champions

Heavyweight Boxing Champion

and here are the Academy Award winners from the year you were born…

_____

Best Picture

_____

Best Director

_____

Best Actor

_____

Best Actress

_____

Best Supporting Actor

_____

Best Supporting Actress

_____

Best Animated Film

_____

Best Foreign Film

When you were born,
the TV news anchors were…

Name, network

Name, network

Name, network

Name, network

Name, network

and the late night talk show hosts were…

Name, network

Name, network

Name, network

Name, network

Name, network

When you were born,
the daytime talk show hosts were…

Name, network

Name, network

Name, network

Name, network

Name, network

and America's Iron Chefs were…

Name, specialty

Name, specialty

Name, specialty

Name, specialty

Name, specialty

When you were born, these celebrities were in the headlines...

Name, reason

Name, reason

Name, reason

Name, reason

Name, reason

Name, reason

Name, reason

Name, reason

Name, reason

Name, reason

When you were born, these were some of the musicians your parents liked...

Musician name

Musician name

Musician name

Musician name

Musician name

and these were some of the movies your parents liked...

Movie name

Movie name

Movie name

Movie name

Movie name

When you were a baby,
you traveled to these places…

City, state, country, date

City, state, country, date

City, state, country, date

City, state, country, date

City, state, country, date

City, state, country, date

City, state, country, date

City, state, country, date

City, state, country, date

City, state, country, date

City, state, country, date

City, state, country, date

City, state, country, date

City, state, country, date

City, state, country, date

City, state, country, date

When you were a baby, some of your favorite bedtime stories were...

Title, author

Title, author

Title, author

Title, author

Title, author

and this is a picture of the one item you couldn't live without...

Place photo here

You first smiled at…

Age

You first rolled over at…

Age

You first crawled at…

Age

Your first tooth came at…

Age

Your first word was…

Word, age

You took your first steps at…

Age

You first slept through the night at…

Age, duration

Your first boo-boo was…

Description, age

A PIC OF YOU AT

1

MONTH OLD

A PIC OF YOU AT

2

MONTHS OLD

A PIC OF YOU AT

3

MONTHS OLD

A PIC OF YOU AT

4

MONTHS OLD

A PIC OF YOU AT

5

MONTHS OLD

A PIC OF YOU AT

6

MONTHS OLD

A PIC OF YOU AT

7

MONTHS OLD

A PIC OF YOU AT

8

MONTHS OLD

A PIC OF YOU AT

9

MONTHS OLD

A PIC OF YOU AT

10

MONTHS OLD

A PIC OF YOU AT

11

MONTHS OLD

A PIC OF YOU AT **12** MONTHS OLD

HAPPY BIRTHDAY TO YOU!

Use these pages for more memories
from your first year . . .

This Is Your Book

by Ryan Maconochie

Published in 2011 by Stewart, Tabori & Chang
An imprint of ABRAMS

Text and illustrations copyright © 2011 Ryan Maconochie

Cataloging-in-Publication Data has been applied for and may be obtained from the Library of Congress.
ISBN: 978-1-58479-948-1

Editor: Wesley Royce
Designer: Ryan Maconochie
Production Manager: Anet Sirna-Bruder

The text of this book was composed in Adobe Caslon.

Printed and bound in China
10 9 8 7 6 5 4 3 2 1

Stewart, Tabori & Chang books are available at special discounts when purchased in quantity for premiums
and promotions as well as fundraising or educational use. Special editions can also be created
to specification. For details, contact specialsales@abramsbooks.com or the address below.

THE ART OF BOOKS SINCE 1949

115 West 18th Street
New York, NY 10011
www.abramsbooks.com